Pathfinder 29

Assessment and planning in the MFL department

Pathfinder

Other titles in the series

Being creative (Barry Jones) PF10

Bridging the gap: GCSE to 'A' level (John Thorogood and Lid King) PF7

Communication re-activated: teaching pupils with learning difficulties (Bernardette Holmes) PF6

Continuous assessment and recording (John Thorogood) PF13

Creative use of texts (Bernard Kavanagh and Lynne Upton) PF21

Departmental planning and schemes of work (Clive Hurren) PF11

Developing skills for independent reading (Iain Mitchell and Ann Swarbrick) PF22

Differentiation (Anne Convery and Do Coyle) PF18

Drama in the languages classroom (Judith Hamilton and Anne McLeod) PF19

Exploring otherness — an approach to cultural awareness (Barry Jones) PF24

Fair enough? Equal opportunities and modern languages (Vee Harris) PF14

Grammar matters (Susan Halliwell) PF17

Improve your image: the effective use of the OHP (Daniel Tierney and Fay Humphreys) PF15

Keeping on target (Bernardette Holmes) PF23

Listening in a foreign language — a skill we take for granted? (Karen Turner) PF26

Making effective use of the dictionary (Gwen Berwick and Phil Horsfall) PF28

Making the case for languages (Alan Moys and Richard Townsend) PF8

New contexts for modern language learning: cross-curricular approaches (Kim Brown and Margot Brown) PF27

Nightshift — ideas and strategies for homework (David Buckland and Mike Short) PF20

Not bothered? Motivating reluctant learners in Key Stage 4 (Jenifer Alison) PF16

On target — teaching in the target language (Susan Halliwell and Barry Jones) PF5

Progressing through the Attainment Targets (Ian Lane) PF12

Reading for pleasure in a foreign language (Ann Swarbrick) PF2

With a song in my scheme of work (Steven Fawkes) PF25

Yes — but will they behave? Managing the interactive classroom (Susan Halliwell) PF4

Pathfinder 29

A CILT series for language teachers

Assessment and planning in the MFL department

Harmer Parr

The views expressed in this publication are the author's and do not necessarily represent those of CILT.

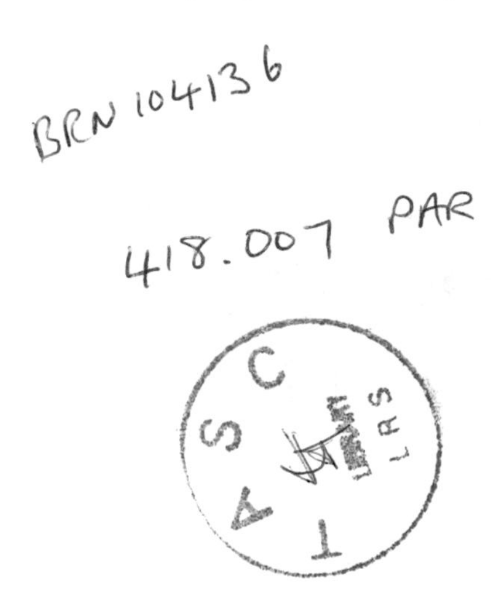

First published in 1997

ISBN 1 874016 71 2

A catalogue record for this book is available from the British Library
Printed in Great Britain by Oakdale Printing Co Ltd

Published by the Centre for Information on Language Teaching and Research,
20 Bedfordbury, Covent Garden, London WC2N 4LB

CILT Publications are available from: Grantham Book Services, Isaac Newton Way, Alma Park Industrial Estate, Grantham, Lincs NG31 8SD. Tel: 01476 567 421. Fax: 01476 590 223. Book trade representation (UK and Ireland): Broadcast Book Services, 24 De Montfort Road, London SW16 1LZ. Tel: 0181 677 5129.

Contents

Introduction

What is assessment for? The problem is that there are too many answers to this question, and they are all right, at least at some point. For example, assessment can be used to:

- help us know what to do next;
- tell us how well we are doing;
- prove to others and ourselves we are doing our job well;
- motivate pupils;
- show improvement;
- create league tables;
- select pupils for groups and sets;
- decide who does a second language . . .

The list is endless, and a second problem is that the categories are not mutually exclusive. The first five, for instance, are all ingredients of the average school report. There are many purposes of assessment, but the key one is to help pupils make progress.

The main purpose of assessment is to improve pupils' learning. Assessment tells the child how well he or she is doing, tells the teacher what needs to be done next and ultimately allows progress to be reported to parents and others. Assessment needs to be accurate, consistent and manageable. Assessments must be valid — they must measure what we believe they measure — and reliable — they must be consistent across teachers and time. Procedures must meet statutory requirements and follow the recommendations of the Special Educational Needs Code of Practice. In all assessment, it is important to measure what we value, or we may only value what we measure.

This book looks at how policies, planning, record keeping, reporting and monitoring can all contribute to that central purpose.

1. Establishing an assessment policy

Assessment policy is usually set within the context of the school's overall policies. At best, department policies have been discussed and agreed by all members of the team.

The following principles should form the basis of any policies on assessing pupils, recording their progress and reporting to parents. Departments could use these to evaluate their current practice and to develop more detailed procedures specific to languages:

Assessment

- Good assessment is based on good planning which identifies expected outcomes and checks if they have been achieved.
- Accurate assessment is promoted by gathering evidence over time and making judgements about it based on clear criteria.
- Assessment techniques should be varied and tailored to what is being assessed: observation, discussion, marking and formal tests all have their place.
- The results of assessment should be used to guide the next steps for teacher and pupil.
- Pupils should know what they are meant to be learning and be encouraged to assess their own progress.
- Oral and written feedback from the teacher should tell pupils how to improve.
- Consistency of judgement should be sought between teachers and between schools to allow pupils to progress smoothly.

Record keeping

- Record keeping should support assessment, not drive it. It should be guided by who, and what, the records are for.

- Records are an evidence base from which information will be taken for different audiences and purposes. Parents have different needs to the pupil's next teacher.

- Records must be manageable and user-friendly: those who need the information should be able to get it when they want, in the form they want, with a minimum of fuss.

- Agreement on standards can be shown by a school or department portfolio. There is no need to compile for moderation purposes separate sets of the work of individual pupils.

- Developing records of achievement with pupils can help to involve and motivate them.

- Too much evidence is as bad as too little.

Reporting

- Reports should sum up the teacher's judgements based on the available evidence.

- Most schools report orally and in writing, and should consider what is best reported when.

- Reports should summarise pupils' strengths and weaknesses against clear criteria and give targets for improvement. It may be better to express a weakness as a target for improvement, but the issue should not be ducked.

- Reports should be clear, positive in tone, and honest. Language used should be free of jargon and accessible to parents and lay readers. Praise is meaningless without the freedom to be critical when necessary.

- All pupils should be encouraged to improve. You don't have to be ill to get better!

You probably found you could agree with most of that. After all, most of us are against sin! The tricky bit is putting these principles into action. Nevertheless, being clear-headed about principles and purposes is an important starting point. One of the clearest manifestations of a department's policy on assessment is to look at the way teachers mark books. Let's try one or two relevant principles.

Marking books

For example:

- Do the criteria for marking reflect the 'expected outcomes' of the exercise?
- Are the criteria clear and explicit?
- Do comments help pupils to know what to do to improve their work next time?
- Is work returned to pupils swiftly enough for comments still to be relevant to them?
- Is everyone using the same system for marking?
- If not, does it matter? Is there a lack of continuity for pupils moving between teachers?

Some of these questions are contentious. If your department has considered them and still not come to blows, you've probably not been concentrating! Try point five (marking systems) for example. Take a selection of exercise books from every teacher in the department, and ask:

- Do we use marks, grades, comments or a combination of all of these?
- Do we use the same approach to the same type of exercise?
- Do we all comment favourably on and reward the same things?
- Is it clear what marks or grades have been given for?
- Is it harder to get a favourable comment from one teacher than another?
- Are comments in the foreign language or English?
- Can pupils understand them?
- Are they told how to make the next piece better?
- Do teachers make use of level descriptions?
- Is there any indication of what the marking criteria are?

You've certainly come to blows now!

Writing a marking policy

A marking policy is a key part of any assessment policy and an ideal way of focusing the mind. You will need, at the very least, to consider the questions above, and several others besides (though not necessarily in this order):

- Do we agree on interpretation of levels of work?
- Are our marks/grades related to criteria or just numerical?
- How do we correct mistakes?
- What comments do we write on pupils' work?
- Do we agree on the relative weighting we give to accuracy and communication?
- Do we mark every exercise the same way?
- Do we respond in different ways to different pupils?
- Do the pupils know what the marking criteria are?
- Are they encouraged to assess their own progress?

Each department must answer these questions for itself. The resulting agreements, when recorded, would constitute a policy which should:

- make a clear statement about the purposes of marking;
- record agreements to the above questions and any others which have arisen in the form of specific operational guidelines;
- review and amend these if necessary in the light of experience.

The nitty gritty — some suggestions

In marking work, teachers often face three apparently incompatible demands. They want to help pupils assess their own progress, they want to make constructive comments and they want to make these in the target language.

At this point, another important principle comes into play: that of using common sense. To start at the end of the above problem, comments should only be in the target language if pupils can understand them! Two solutions suggest themselves, bearing in mind the key purpose of assessment, to improve pupils' work. Firstly, if something important needs to be said and that something would be incomprehensible in the target language, say it in English. Secondly, explore ways of making more comments understood in the target language.

A starting point can be the use of comment and statement banks of a multiple choice variety. For example, many reading schemes now have built-in evaluation techniques:

J'ai trouvé ce livre	**Ich fand es**
❑ intéressant	❑ relativ interessant
❑ ennuyeux	❑ sehr interessant
❑ difficile	❑ ergreifend
❑ facile	❑ tragisch

Such expressions are first recognised, (the appropriate item or box is ticked), and then used by pupils, firstly in answer to the teacher's question and then independently in speech and writing. The number and complexity of responses increase as the pupils progress, and some build a large, active vocabulary, with which they can discuss their reading.

A similar approach is possible to self-assessment by pupils and to comments by the teacher. Starting with a small bank of comments, the repertoire can be developed and extended. It is a key way in which pupils can express views and opinions:

> *J'ai bien/très bien travaillé; j'ai tout compris, je n'ai rien compris; j'ai eu neuf sur dix; j'ai trouvé cet exercice trop difficile/très facile*

The teacher encourages pupils to use these phrases orally and in writing on self-assessment sheets, and incorporates them in comments on written work:

> *Tu as très bien travaillé,* etc.

At a more sophisticated level, criteria from the level descriptions can be introduced in the target language and pupils can be encouraged to use them in their self-assessments. Qualifiers like *manchmal, de vez en cuando, siempre, le plus souvent,* etc can be used to increase the range of expression:

> *Je comprends les instructions simples de temps en temps/souvent/toujours*
> *Je réponds immédiatement aux questions simples*
> *Je sais dire ce que j'aime/je n'aime pas*
> *Je copie les phrases simples sans erreur*

As before, pupils move from recognising these items to producing them for themselves. It is rare, though not unheard of, for pupils to have developed an impressive stock of vocabulary for evaluating their own work and that of others by the time they reach Key Stage 4. Free expression in the target language has to start somewhere, and pupils will not produce what they have not been taught.

2. Assessment and planning

The National Curriculum Programmes of Study are, of course, the starting point for planning — at least theoretically. In practice, the starting point for the teacher is often the course book used. The Programmes of Study serve more as a template which is used to evaluate schemes of work to ensure that all the listed opportunities of Part 1 and areas of Part 2 are covered. Once a term or so, it is useful for a department to reflect on Part 1 of the programme of study and consider if all opportunities are being provided. Do current course materials allow this? If not, are new materials required, or is it a question of new approaches with existing resources? Is everyone agreed about what the statements actually mean?

The level descriptions also have their place in planning. Firstly, they can be used in longer term planning. For example, in Year 7, the majority of pupils will probably be working between levels 1 and 3. The teacher can use the level descriptions at the start of the year to gain a firm idea of the range of expected performance. This template can also be applied to the course materials — for example, in writing, are there opportunities for above average pupils to write short phrases from memory, to express personal responses, to write two or three sentences about familiar topics, etc? If not, how can the course materials be supplemented? Are pupils reading independently, selecting their own texts, using bilingual dictionaries? It is too late to discover in Year 9 that they need to!

Secondly, in unit, weekly and daily planning it is necessary to plan for outcomes which will usually be related to skills described in the level descriptions. The generalised statements of the descriptors have to be related to the content of the topic in hand:

For example, in a Year 7 topic:

- Which 'single words and short phrases' will pupils be producing in this unit?
- Which 'short, simple responses' will be expected?
- What does the restaurant scene with 'at least two or three exchanges' sound like? etc.

One problem of the level descriptions is that they are somewhat unwieldy for planning purposes. A solution to this is to simplify them, for operational purposes only, concentrating on the key elements of progression. In all four attainment targets, the elements of progression can be summarised under three headings:

- the complexity of the task or text (to include spoken 'text');
- the complexity of the response expected;
- the degree of independence implied/support required.

In other words, in deciding on the relative difficulty of activities, you will need to consider the following questions (examples drawn from level descriptions):

How difficult is the text?

- If it is a listening text, is it simple, containing short sentences with no interference, or more complex, containing wide-ranging subject material, complex sentences, background noise, native-speaker speed of delivery, etc?
- If it is a reading text, is the language familiar, is there a range of tense and vocabulary, is it abstract, etc?

How difficult is the task?

- Does it require the production of single words, short phrases, whole sentences?
- Does it require the identification of abstract notions?
- Does it involve unpredictability, etc?

The difficulty of the activity will depend on the interplay of text and task. It is possible to set a simple task on a difficult text, and vice versa. In general, the difficulty of listening and reading tasks will depend mainly on the complexity of the text.

How complex is the required response?

- Do pupils have to identify factual details or abstract notions?
- Is the meaning stated or does it have to be inferred?
- Does it involve expressing opinions, linking ideas, using tenses? etc.

How much support is given?

- Do pupils have to use their own knowledge of language to work out meaning/adapt phrases?
- What clues/cues/help are given?
- Are reference materials available? etc.

Complexity of response and degree of support will be the main determinants of difficulty in speaking and writing tasks.

In all four skills, as support decreases, the need for independence increases.

The simplified version of the level descriptions looks like the examples on the following pages:

ATTAINMENT TARGET 1: LISTENING

Level	Task/Text	Response	Independence
EP	◆ wide range ◆ factual and imaginative issues and concerns	◆ summarise in detail ◆ report and explain in speech and writing	◆ select according to interest
8	◆ range of types and sources ◆ interviews, documentaries, films, plays	◆ infer meaning ◆ recognise attitudes and emotions	
7	◆ complex sentences ◆ unfamiliar language ◆ news items		
6	◆ short narratives ◆ unfamiliar contexts ◆ opinions ◆ normal speed ◆ some interference	◆ identify points of view	◆ need little repetition
5	◆ range of topics ◆ past, present, future	◆ identify opinions	
4	◆ longer passages ◆ simple sentences ◆ little interference	◆ identify other specific details	◆ some repetition
3	◆ short passages ◆ near normal speed	◆ identify main points ◆ give personal responses	◆ repetition of sections
2	◆ longer utterances		◆ repetition
1	◆ simple, short utterances ◆ familiar ◆ no interference	◆ show understanding by picture, word or deed	◆ considerable support ◆ repetition ◆ clues

ATTAINMENT TARGET 2: SPEAKING

Level	Task/Text	Response	Independence
EP	◆ wide range of factual and imaginative topics ◆ formal and informal	◆ discuss topics ◆ give/seek views ◆ fluent ◆ consistently accurate ◆ vary intonation	◆ clear messages ◆ few errors
8	◆ unpredictable elements ◆ unfamiliar people	◆ discuss facts, ideas, experiences ◆ range of vocab, structure ◆ range of time reference	◆ confident ◆ few mistakes
7	◆ personal/topical interest ◆ some unprepared situations	◆ give/ justify opinions ◆ adapt language to situation ◆ accurate ◆ good pronunciation ◆ good intonation	◆ readily understood
6	◆ conversations with past, present, future ◆ some unpredictability	◆ develop conversations ◆ improvise and paraphrase ◆ use TL for routine needs	◆ some hesitation ◆ maintain conversation
5	◆ short conversations ◆ simple language ◆ recent past, present, future ◆ everyday activities and interests	◆ seek and give information	◆ make self understood ◆ some mistakes
4	◆ minimum three or four exchanges ◆ structured	◆ adapt/substitute words and phrases ◆ accurate pronunciation and intonation	◆ use knowledge of language to adapt
3	◆ exchanges ◆ short sentences/phrases	◆ initiate and respond ◆ simple likes/dislikes ◆ substitute vocabulary to vary	◆ visual and other cues ◆ mainly memorised phrases
2		◆ name/describe people, places, objects ◆ set phrases ◆ some hesitation	◆ ask for help/permission
1	◆ straightforward	◆ single word ◆ short phrase	◆ considerable support ◆ imitate a model

ATTAINMENT TARGET 3: READING

Level	Task/Text	Response	Independence
EP	◆ wide range of factual and imaginative texts ◆ points of view, issues and concerns	◆ summarise in detail ◆ report, explain ◆ orally and in writing	◆ select and respond to stories, articles, books, plays
8	◆ unfamiliar topics ◆ variety of types ◆ complex language	◆ read for personal interest and information ◆ recognise attitudes, emotions	◆ consult range of reference sources
7	◆ imaginative and factual texts ◆ some complex and unfamiliar language	◆ use reading to support speaking and writing	◆ select and use reference materials
6	◆ variety of texts ◆ includes unfamiliar contexts ◆ magazines, stories	◆ identify/note points of view ◆ scan	◆ select texts ◆ use context and grammar to deduce meaning
5	◆ range of material ◆ includes authentic texts ◆ past, present, future events	◆ identify/note opinions	◆ use reference materials ◆ confident in reading aloud
4	◆ short stories ◆ factual texts ◆ printed or clearly handwritten	◆ identify/note other details	◆ begin to use context to deduce meaning
3	◆ short texts/dialogues ◆ familiar language	◆ identify/note main points	◆ select simple texts ◆ use bilingual dictionary or glossary
2	◆ short phrases ◆ familiar context, words and phrases	◆ match sound to print ◆ read aloud	◆ use books and glossaries to find new words
1	◆ single words ◆ familiar context ◆ clear script	◆ show understanding	◆ visual support

ATTAINMENT TARGET 4: WRITING

Level	Task/Text	Response	Independence
EP	◆ wide range of factual and imaginative topics	◆ write coherently and accurately	◆ use resources to vary style and scope ◆ match form and style to task
8	◆ longer sequences	◆ express/justify/seek points of view ◆ develop content of material read or heard	◆ accurate spelling, grammar ◆ match style to content ◆ use reference to improve and extend
7	◆ texts of varying lengths ◆ real and imaginary subjects	◆ link sentences/paragraphs ◆ structure ideas ◆ adapt to purpose ◆ edit and re-draft	◆ use reference sources to achieve accuracy, precision, variety ◆ occasional mistakes
6	◆ paragraphs ◆ past, present, future ◆ formal/informal	◆ use simple, descriptive language	◆ clear meaning ◆ some mistakes
5	◆ short, simple pieces ◆ recent experience ◆ present activities ◆ future plans	◆ seek/give information and opinions	◆ begin to apply grammar in new contexts ◆ use dictionaries ◆ some mistakes
4	◆ short paragraphs of three or four simple sentences	◆ adapt by substituting words and set phrases	◆ memorised language ◆ use dictionaries and glossaries
3	◆ short sentences ◆ familiar topics	◆ write short phrases from memory ◆ express likes, dislikes, feelings	◆ understandable spelling ◆ use books, textbooks, displays for reference
2	◆ write or word process	◆ copy familiar phrases correctly ◆ write words from memory	◆ approximate spelling when writing from memory
1	◆ straightforward	◆ copy single, familiar words correctly ◆ label ◆ select words to complete sentences	◆ considerable support

4. Using assessment information in the department

The central message of this book has been that the key to good planning is good assessment: knowing exactly where your pupils are allows you to set appropriate goals for them. This is true at individual level but also at the level of the department. There is a strong emphasis currently on monitoring and evaluation: monitoring to check that what you think is happening is in fact happening, and evaluating the quality of what you do using some pre-agreed criteria.

Monitoring

We have already touched on monitoring: for example, agreeing your definitions of the opportunities and content of the national curriculum programmes of study and checking you are providing them. As with all assessment, the important thing is to act on what you find. If pupils are not:

taking part in imaginative and creative activities, e.g. improvised drama

why is this? What prevents you from doing it? How could you do it? Do you need additional resources? etc.

In addition to monitoring your **coverage of the national curriculum**, you will wish to check if your **policies** are being implemented. Does the department have a policy on 'using the target language'? If so, are teachers doing what has been agreed? If not, is the policy unrealistic? Do teachers need some in-service work? Does the policy need to be changed or updated?

A third area of monitoring will be **examination results**. The educational arena is now awash with statistics which can help you make comparisons with local and national figures and also with other departments in the school. Most schools see the analysis of examination data as a key part of their school improvement strategy. It is particularly important to analyse the points breakdown provided by GCSE examination boards. Why, for example, did no pupil score more than 1 point on Higher Level writing, or why did no pupil gain 4 points in Basic Level listening?

It is appropriate to add one or two caveats at this point. Firstly, bear in mind our key principle to *measure what you value or you will only value what you measure*. Examination results provide one view of a department's performance, but there are others. Secondly, there is a danger of crunching so many numbers that the wood gets lost in the trees ('Too much information is as bad as too little.'). Decide first what it is important to know and focus on that (key principle: what is it for?). Thirdly, do not be beguiled into thinking that analysis of exam results, on its own, gives you the answers to your questions. What it does is throw up questions which need to be explored and tested. There may be a simple explanation of why the lower attaining pupils did so much worse this year. The fact that their teacher broke her neck and the supply teacher only turned up once could have a bearing on the matter!

Comparing your results with those of other schools

National statistics are available for the percentage of pupils achieving A*–C and A*–G grades, and for the average points score of candidates (calculated on basis of A* = 8, A = 7, B = 6, C = 5, etc. divided by the number of candidates entered). National figures are calculated on the basis of the number of candidates entered for the exam. It is worth calculating as well A*–C and A*–G grades as a percentage of the total number of pupils in the year. This gives a constant point of comparison year on year and does not have the disadvantages of fluctuating entry and year group sizes. Most LEAs also publish local statistics, so it is now possible to compare how well you are doing with schools locally and nationally.

The next question, of course, is 'so what?'. To compare schools with each other in the ways described usually tells us what we already knew: Leafy Suburbs Grammar School has results above local and national averages. Gasworks Secondary Modern is below. It is far more useful to attempt to compare like with like — for example by taking account of the intake characteristics of the school, or by comparing the performance of the same pupils in all their subjects.

Some schools use externally produced data (e.g. ALIS and YELLIS). SCAA is exploring the possibility of introducing 'value-added' approaches more widely. A 'value-added' approach is one where characteristics of the pupils on entry to the school are used to calculate a starting point against which future performance is measured. Up to now, features such as the percentage of pupils in the school eligible for free school meals have been aggregated to arrive at a kind of deprivation or advantage quotient. Increasingly, these are being replaced by measures of 'prior attainment'. Already, statistics exist in English, Maths and Science for seven-, eleven- and fourteen-year-olds based on national assessments and tests. Baseline assessments on entry to school are being actively considered. These 'benchmarks' can be used to calculate the 'value added' by a school or subject.

Many schools are already using measures such as these to calculate their performance against other similar schools, and to compare the performance of subject departments. A pupil's points score in, say, German, can be compared with the average points score of the same pupil in her or his other subjects. The difference is usually expressed as a plus or minus, called a 'residual'. For example:

Sharon Smith: Points score in French: 7 (grade A); average points score in all other subjects 6.5; residual +0.5.

What this shows is that Sharon Smith achieved half a grade better in French than in her other subjects. By doing this calculation for all pupils taking French, a 'subject residual' can be derived, telling a department how well it is performing in examination results compared with other subjects in the same school. National residual figures are also available. These show that French is, in fact, slightly harder than other subjects, making the above achievement all the more impressive. Had the national residual also been +0.5, Sharon's achievement would have been in line with that of other pupils nationally, and therefore less remarkable. Schools which have been inspected since September 1996 will have received data such as this in their pre-inspection reports (PICSI) from OFSTED.

Monitoring results is an important part of schools' work today. The key question, as always, is how you use the information to improve things next time round. The aim is continuous improvement — you don't have to be ill to get better.

Evaluating standards in the department

Monitoring results is one way of knowing how you are doing as a department. Another is to use the criteria of the national curriculum to evaluate the standards of work in the early secondary years.

One of the most useful activities a department can engage in is to look at and listen to samples of written and spoken work and reach collective agreements about standards.

A department can agree interpretations of national curriculum levels by applying them to the work of selected pupils. Bear in mind that ultimately it is pupils, not individual pieces of work, that are 'levelled' and one piece on its own does not constitute evidence that the pupil always performs at that level. It is very useful to look at selected work from pupils of differing levels of attainment and considering best-fit judgements in the way described in SCAA's *Exemplification of standards*. It is also useful, with the above proviso, to select for moderation purposes some pieces of work which exemplify a typical performance at a certain level.

When good examples have been found, they can be collected together into a department 'portfolio', annotated appropriately. It is useful, for example, if a particular piece has provoked a lively debate, to include a brief resume of the discussion and conclusions for future reference. A well-constructed portfolio, containing a few, carefully chosen, illustrative pieces can serve a number of purposes. For example, it can tell new staff, students, visitors or inspectors what standards you are applying. But most of all it can be a permanent record of probably the most important discussions you will have.

Another important activity based on the portfolio is that of considering how well your standards compare with external expectations. In national tests in the core subjects of English, Maths and Science, just under 60% of Year 9 pupils have attained Level 5 and just under 30% Level 6. Teacher assessments in the foundation subjects in which there are levels are expected to show a similar picture in 1997, though the later start in languages (still usually at age eleven) may have an effect on this. As a rough guide, it is suggested that the levels achieved by an average attaining pupil nationally are:

Year 7: level 2 (main range 1–3)
Year 8: levels 3/4 (main range 2–5)
Year 9: levels 4/5 (main range 3–6)

Using these as a guide, you can assess how well your pupils are performing compared to these national 'benchmarks'. If your school has data on the characteristics of pupils on entry to the school (i.e. average, above average or below average profile) you can further assess whether your standards are about what should be expected. Don't forget to check that there is progression in skills as well as content from year to year.

Ofsted inspectors will do all this to you. There is nothing to stop you doing it first! Having made judgements yourselves about where you stand and having evidence on which to base those judgements are very good bases for discussion with outsiders — whoever they are!

Having a clear idea of where you are is a sound basis for setting targets for improvement. Targets based on careful assessment have a much better chance of success, and it is no use having the data if you do not use them to move forward. For some good ideas, try the DfEE/OFSTED publication *Setting targets to raise standards* mentioned in the Bibliography on p33.

Conclusion

This book has looked at a range of aspects of assessment related to individuals, the department and the school. The section on policy suggested a framework of principles and questions on which good assessment should be based. Planning, record keeping, reporting, monitoring and evaluation were all then related to those principles. Of all the questions posed, the key one, and the starting point for all subsequent questions, is essentially a simple one: 'what's it for?' Being clear about that before you take any further steps is the surest way to ensure that your efforts do bring about real benefits for your pupils. Good luck!

Bibliography and further reading

Assessment, recording and reporting, Key Stages 1, 2 and 3, Fourth Year 1992/93 (OFSTED/HMSO, 1994)

Assessment, recording and reporting, Third Year 1991/92 (OFSTED/HMSO, 1993)

The implementation of the Code of Practice for pupils with SEN (OFSTED/HMSO, 1996)

Key Stage 3 optional tests and tasks — modern foreign languages (SCAA/ACAC, 1996)

MFL: a review of inspection findings 1993/94 (OFSTED/HMSO, 1995)

MFL: exemplification of standards (SCAA/ACAC, 1996)

MFL non-statutory guidance (National Curriculum Council, 1992)

MFL in the National Curriculum (DFE, 1995)

Promoting high achievement for pupils with SEN in mainstream schools (OFSTED/HMSO, 1996)

Reporting pupils' achievements (OFSTED/HMSO, 1995)

Setting targets to raise standards: a survey of good practice (OFSTED/DfEE, 1996)

If there is no entry in a box, the previous, lower-level statement still applies. This is to maintain a focus on those elements which make one level different from another. It is important to remember that this simplified model is no substitute for the level descriptions themselves. The main use of level descriptions is to make 'best-fit' judgements about the work of individual pupils over a period of time. The only statutory requirement is to make this best-fit judgement at the end of Key Stage 3. Schools may decide to use level descriptions for summative purposes at other points in the course, and can decide whether or not they wish to share this information with parents. This point is dealt with more fully in the section on reporting. The above model is for use in planning as a simple memory jogger of the key elements of progression. The table opposite demonstrates how the model works in Year 7, by showing the range of expected performance:

When applied to a specific unit on the family, this means that, as a minimum, by the end of the unit:

All pupils can (with support if necessary):

- understand the words for key members of the family when heard or seen;
- introduce members of the family (*Voici mon père, Hier ist meine Mutter, Es mi hermano,* etc), e.g. when talking about photographs;
- copy these words correctly, e.g. when labelling a family photograph.

And additionally, some pupils can:

- pick out those key words in longer sentences with repetition if necessary;
- give their names/ages (*se llama___, tiene 14 anos,* etc);
- look up words in the glossary;
- ask for help in target language;
- read the words aloud;
- write them from memory with reasonable accuracy.

And additionally, some pupils can:

- understand family details in short tape-recorded passages;
- ask and answer questions about the family (*Qui est-ce?, comment s'appelle . . ?, quel âge a . . ?,* etc, sustaining a short conversation;
- select readers, read short texts about the family;
- look up words in a dictionary;
- write short sentences about the family from memory: *Mein Bruder heißt Hans. Er ist zwölf Jahre alt. Er spielt gern Fußball.*

Year 7, mixed-ability class
Topic of 'my family'

Longer-term planning:

Range of expected outcomes (mainly levels 1–3, some pupils at 4?):

	LISTENING	SPEAKING	READING	WRITING
Most able	deal with longer passages and cope with a little interference	manage at least three or four exchanges, adapting and substituting words and phrases	read short stories and factual texts; begin to use context to deduce meaning	write short paragraphs of three or four sentences, adapting and using dictionaries and glossaries
Above average	identify points and give personal responses in short passages at near normal speed	initiate and respond in short exchanges, using visual cues and memorised language	read short texts and dialogues, identifying main points; select texts and use a bilingual dictionary	write short sentences on familiar topics, short phrases from memory with understandable spelling; use reference materials
Average	deal with longer utterances, still needing repetition	use set phrases to name and describe people, places, objects and ask for help and permission	read short phrases, read aloud, use books and glossaries to find words	copy phrases correctly and write words from memory with approximate spelling
Below average	understand short, simple utterances of familiar language with no interference and considerable support	deal with straight-forward tasks producing single words and short phrases with considerable support	understand single words in a familiar context and clear script, with support	deal with straight-forward tasks, selecting and copying single words correctly, with considerable support

And additionally, a few pupils can:

- understand taped extracts with a little interference;
- take part in a conversation about the family with at least three or four exchanges;
- work out the meaning of longer texts/short stories, using the context to guess sensibly;
- write short paragraphs about their and other people's families, with reasonable accuracy.

In planning for this range of attainment in a mixed-ability Year 7 class, the teacher cannot, of course, plan four different sets of lessons. In practice, the input will be broadly similar for all and differentiation will be achieved partly by different tasks but mainly by the outcome expected. In other words, there will be an initial presentation of new vocabulary and phrases and practice of them, followed by common activities where differentiation will be achieved by the amount and quality of language produced (least able match words to pictures, most able encouraged to write three or four sentences about each picture etc.), followed by further activities which allow pupils to work at an appropriate level (fast finishers given a more difficult tape or longer writing exercise).

The main concern is to be sure that the activities planned do make it possible to achieve the expected range of levels. Sometimes, the most practical way of managing this is to start at the end: with the expected maximum outcome. In our example, it may be that we would expect our above average group to produce the following language in speech and writing:

> *Bonjour. Je m'appelle Marie. J'ai onze ans. J'ai un frère et deux soeurs. Mon frère s'appelle Andrew et mes soeurs s'appellent Nicola et Tracey. Andrew et Nicola sont plus jeunes que moi. Andrew a huit ans et Nicola a quatre ans. Tracey a dix-huit ans. Ma mère est institutrice et mon père est au chômage.*

The pupils would also be able to ask the relevant questions in the above.

In working with the above core of language, the expectation is that the most able pupils, eventually, produce all of it accurately in speech and writing. The least able understand all the key words, and can answer most of the questions, albeit monosyllabically:

> *Comment t'appelles-tu? Marie*
> *Quel âge a Tracey? Dix-huit ans,* etc.

Planning for the unit is then directed at the end point (the 'end of unit goal' — see *MFL non-statutory guidance,* Section G, NCC 1992). The reason for learning the questions and answers could be, for instance, 'making materials to send to French link class'. Pupils have real questions to ask, real answers to give and a reason to do it. If you do not have a link class in France, there should be one just down the corridor. This activity is a good way of helping Year 7 classes to get to know each other. Alternatively, since families are sometimes best avoided (!), fictitious families based on role play cards can be the basis of some wonderful soap-operas. Why not create your own 'street' or block of flats where the characters created have their own likes, dislikes, foibles and ongoing adventures? After all, your pupils will probably go home to watch *Eastenders,* so why not let them create their own version first? Their fictitious street may be much better than the real thing!

Once the end of unit goal is established and made specific, planning is directed at that outcome. Elements are practised and grammar is reinforced in a meaningful context. This unit provides an ideal opportunity to teach and re-inforce *mon/ma/mes,* etc, and accuracy in speech and writing will depend on it. It is difficult, for instance, to give a decent commentary in French on your family photos without some understanding of *mon/ma/mes:*

> *Voici mon père: il s'appelle . . . ; voici ma mère: elle s'appelle . . . ; voici mon chien: il est mignon; voici mes poissons rouges: ils sont stupides,* etc.

The photo scenario may be just the context you need to explore your genders, personal pronouns and possessive adjectives!

PLANNING FOR PUPILS WITH SPECIAL EDUCATIONAL NEEDS

The Code of Practice on the Identification and Assessment of Pupils with Special Educational Needs came into force from September 1994. Schools are required to 'have regard to the Code' and to 'plan their provision in the light of the Code', though they have discretion about how to do it. The best-known aspect of the Code has been the introduction of five stages from the initial registering of a concern (stage 1) to the preparation of a statement of special educational need (stages 4 and 5). For the classroom teacher, the key change is the introduction of individual education plans (IEPs) for pupils from stage 2 onwards. IEPs typically list the areas of concern and then propose targets for meeting the stated needs. Usually, these needs and targets are not subject-specific, and have to be interpreted.

Schools have many different ways of implementing the Code of Practice guidelines, and it is beyond the scope of this book to dwell on organisational matters. Suffice it to say that there needs to be close liaison between the subject department and the SEN department to ensure that provision is coherent and well targeted at the pupil's needs. Good IEPs are usually a reflection of well-managed collaboration, which includes an indication, at subject level, of the kinds of activities likely to be successful with individuals or groups.

EDUCATION PLANS

It is worth dwelling on the characteristics of a good IEP, because they are no different from those of a good lesson plan. The secret is to have targets which can pass the SMART analysis test, in other words, they are:

S pecific
M easurable
A ttainable
R elevant
T ime-related

In a poorly constructed plan, targets such as: 'improve listening skills' are not developed beyond this bald statement. There are several problems with this, as a glance at our assessment principles would show. We do not know what to do, how to do it, by when, what constitutes success or how we would know if we had succeeded. In fact, we shall never succeed because we can always improve! The pupil will be demoralised, rather than motivated by our plan, as the same target will be repeated year after year. Different teachers will interpret the instruction in different ways, so treatment will not be consistent. In short, the target is not specific, measurable, attainable, relevant or time-related, and is unlikely to be of any use whatever.

Obviously, the need to 'improve listening skills' has to be broken down [illegible] interpreted at subject level. Targets meeting the SMART criteria could be, for instance:

Targets for week beginning _____/for Monday/for end of unit (as appropriate)

1. Recognise five words connected with current topic (e.g. 'house and home') when spoken by the teacher.
2. Recognise the same five words in a short sentence spoken by the teacher, etc.

These would be followed by an indication of the activities which will be used to meet the targets.

These targets are realistic and both teacher and pupil can know when they have been achieved. Progress can be demonstrated.

This 'small steps' approach is particularly effective for pupils with learning difficulties. However, the basic technique of setting goals which are specific, measurable, attainable, relevant and time-related is appropriate for all types of lesson planning. The objectives for a well-planned lesson should be just as clear. For this reason, many teachers view their lesson plans as, effectively, a Group Education Plan. Some departments use GEPs very successfully, particularly with groups of slow learners. Some advantages are:

- lesson objectives are specific;
- they can be easily shared with pupils;
- success is visible and immediate;
- rewards can be related to the achievement of targets.

The last point is especially worth bearing in mind where pupils have behavioural difficulties. Such pupils usually respond well to tangible rewards related to what they have achieved. An approach which positively rewards achievement will be more effective in the long term than one where rewards are related to the avoidance of bad behaviour.

3. Keeping records

Statutory requirements for record keeping are now minimal: schools have almost infinite discretion as long as they can:

- make a best-fit judgement for each pupil at the end of KS3;
- show there is some basis for the judgement.

In judging the quality of procedures, inspectors would try to establish whether assessments made were:

- accurate;
- consistent;
- used.

Accuracy and consistency are closely linked. Assessments are more likely to be accurate if teachers have agreed their interpretation of levels and related their standards to those proposed in the SCAA Exemplification materials. Where this has happened, teachers in a department will probably be applying consistent standards and those standards are more likely to be in line with those in other schools. But the key element is that assessment is used to improve pupils' learning, in other words that the strengths and weaknesses identified by assessment form the basis of the next steps for a particular pupil or class.

WHAT RECORDS SHOULD TEACHERS KEEP TO MEET THESE PURPOSES?

Records will reflect the approach to planning: 'identify expected outcomes' (planning) and 'check they have been achieved' (assessment). Teachers need to record this progress on a day-to-day basis to allow overall judgements to be made when they are needed. As a reminder, our principles of record keeping included being clear about who and what the records are for and having them in a format which allows quick retrieval. Teachers will **wish** to reflect regularly on pupils' progress. Depending on internal school systems, they will **have** to review progress at least once a year, for reporting purposes, and probably a good deal more often for other reasons (e.g. half-termly progress reports, etc). Reasons for reviewing progress include:

- to set targets for pupils;
- to gather information for reports;
- to summarise information for the next teacher.

Day-to-day records

These will usually be kept in the teacher's register and can be in any format which suits the teacher. The key requirement is that essential information can be retrieved from them quickly and summarised when needed. Therefore, it makes no difference whether marks, grades or comments are used, **provided the criteria are clear.**

For example, a listening task can involve the kinds of skills required at level 3. In other words, it is a tape of short conversations at near normal speed where pupils have to pick out specific details. If there are 20 such details, a mark out of 20 may well be appropriate. Provided the register indicates that the activity is 'level 3' (i.e. the kind of activity where successful completion would be characteristic of a 'level 3 pupil', since ultimately it is pupils, not activities, who are 'levelled') then a mark of 18 out of 20 is a powerful piece of evidence, as, perish the thought, is a mark of 2 out of 20. Where a speaking or writing activity offers a range of possible outcomes, this range can be indicated at the head of the column and the marks related to the levels or the levels themselves can be directly recorded.

For continuity, it is important for teachers within a department to adopt a common approach. Some departments prefer to standardise by having a common grading system, using, for instance, a four-point scale for all marking. The department then either draws up criteria for each point which can be used across the age range, e.g.:

- meets all the requirements of the task;
- meets most of the requirements, etc;

or alternatively relates the four point scale to the predominant range of national curriculum levels for the age group. In the case of the Year 7 referred to earlier, the four levels could relate to the four identified in the table on p16. This is then adjusted upwards in each succeeding year. In Key Stage 4, levels can be related to GCSE outcomes taken from the relevant grade criteria.

In judging what is best for your department, you should consider what information will help to sum up progress against national curriculum, GCSE and other relevant criteria with a minimum of extra work and fuss. Day-to-day notes are 'field notes' for use by the individual teacher, but a well-conceived, common approach will cut down the work load for everyone. It is not suggested that every activity, or even most activities, need to be assessed in the way described above. Your records should be a check on the activities covered, their purpose and a mark or grade related to it which allows a profile of each pupil to be built up and acted upon. Your knowledge of the pupil will always supplement any records kept. For example, that string of zeros in the vocabulary tests may be a pupil who cannot write words from memory or one who never does his homework!

Whatever system you use, you should ensure that:

- you know where each pupil is, what they can do, what they cannot do;
- you use this information to remedy weaknesses or to move pupils to the next stage;
- the information you record is useful to you and ultimately in a form to be useful to the pupil's next teacher.

REVIEWING PROGRESS

As indicated at the start of this section, you need to summarise your assessment information from time to time. One possible approach which avoids duplication of effort is to use the appropriate range of (simplified) level descriptions for the class (e.g. 1–4 in the Year 7 example on p15). Pull these together on to a single sheet for each pupil, and use a highlighter to show your current, best-fit judgement. This is a quick way of seeing present strengths and weaknesses and establishing targets for individual pupils. At the end of the year, the completed sheets can be used to write reports and then be passed on to the next teacher.

The following is a highlighted example for Michelle, a Year 7 pupil. Michelle's report, based on this review, is shown in the next section.

(Michelle is a fictitious pupil and her profile is tidier than it might be in 'real life'. Her current working level is Level 2, although she shows some Level 3 characteristics, which are not yet sufficiently consolidated to be reported to parents.)

	AT1: Listening	AT2: Speaking	AT3: Reading	AT4: Writing
Level 4	deal with longer passages and cope with a little interference	manage at least 3/4 exchanges, adapting and substituting words and phrases	read short stories and factual texts; begin to use context to deduce meaning	write short paragraphs of 3/4 sentences, adapting and using dictionaries and glossaries
Level 3	identify points and give personal responses in short passages at near normal speed	initiate and respond in short exchanges, using visual cues and memorised language	read short texts and dialogues, identifying main points; select texts and use a bilingual dictionary	write short sentences on familiar topics, short phrases from memory with understandable spelling; use reference materials
Level 2	deal with longer utterances, still needing repetition	use set phrases to name and describe people, places, objects and ask for help and permission	read short phrases, read aloud, use books and glossaries to find words	copy phrases correctly and write words from memory with approximate spelling
Level 1	understand short, simple utterances of familiar language with no interference and considerable support	deal with straightforward tasks producing single words and short phrases with considerable support	understand single words in a familiar context and clear script, with support	deal with straightforward tasks, selecting and copying single words correctly, with considerable support